A FIRE IN THE HEAD

ALSO BY ANDREW FITZSIMONS:

What the Sky Arranges: Poems made from the Tsurezuregusa *of Kenkō* (Isobar Press, 2013)

The Sea of Disappointment: Thomas Kinsella's Pursuit of the Real (University College Dublin Press, 2008)

EDITED BY ANDREW FITZSIMONS:

Thomas Kinsella, *Prose Occasions 1951-2006* (Carcanet, 2009)

A FIRE IN THE HEAD

震災後にこしらえたハイク

ANDREW FITZSIMONS

Drawings by Sergio Maria Calatroni

Japanese translations by
Nobuaki Tochigi & Mitsuko Ohno

ISOBAR PRESS

First published in 2014 by

Isobar Press
Sakura 2-21-23-202
Setagaya-ku
Tokyo 156-0053
Japan

http://isobarpress.com

ISBN 978-4-907359-06-5

English text © Andrew Fitzsimons, 2014
Haiku translations © Nobuaki Tochigi, 2014
Essay translation © Mitsuko Ohno. 2014
Drawings © Sergio Maria Calatroni, 2014

All rights reserved.

Acknowledgements

Acknowledgement is due to the editors of *Gendaishitecho* (Journal of Contemporary Poetry) in which an abbreviated version of *A Fire in the Head* first appeared, in English and Japanese.

'What are Poets for?...' first appeared in the *Japan Mission Journal* Vol. 65, No. 2 (Summer 2011). A special thanks to Joseph S. O'Leary.

A Fire in the Head

Contents

I

A Fire in the Head　　　13

II

'What Are Poets for?'…　　　61

「詩人は何のために？」…　　　76

for Gerald Dawe

I went out to the hazel wood,
Because a fire was in my head…

       W. B. Yeats

私はハシバミの森へ行った
頭にひとつ炎が灯ったので

       W・B・イェイツ

A tunnel. Train tracks.
Into the living room, out.
Around and around.

トンネルくぐり線路居間へ入り出てぐるりぐるり

Traditionally
on this day winter begins.
Traditionally.

暦の上では今日からが冬
暦の上では今日からが

Oranges glisten
in the sunlight after rain.
Our neighbour's garden.

雨上がりの陽を浴びて隣の庭の蜜柑が艶めく

All those cabbages
about to be de-headed.
The caterpillar?

今まさにキャベツ打ち首にされんとする畑に一匹の青虫

Faults, temblors, epicentres, moment magnitudes. The catfish. The stone.

断層震動震源モーメントマグニチュード鯰要石

Flight to higher ground;
sparrows in a leafless tree;
the furies and fates.

高台へ避難裸木に雀すずめ復讐の女神運命の女神

Zelkova branches:
ramifying through spaces
in the eye, the mind.

ケヤキの木が枝々を広げる目の中で心の中で

Silver bicycle
outside a supermarket –
leaves in its basket.

スーパーの前に銀色の自転車―籠の中には落ち葉たち

Ka-ka-ka, the crow.
Chun-chun chun-chun, the sparrow.
An open window.

かあかあカラスちゅんちゅん雀窓は開いています

From the North Country:
children with faraway eyes,
gazing out to sea.

『北の国から』――子どもらが遠い目で海原を見つめている

The field, the farmer:
a head of cabbage in hand.
Weighing. Weighed. Weighing.

畑にて農家の人の掌でキャベツの頭が量り量られ量り

U.S. aeroplanes
on recce from Yokota,
in V formation.

アメリカ軍偵察機群横田基地発V字編隊

Sere, the yellow leaf:
the Ginkgo lording over
the Paulownia.

黄色い乾(ひ)反(そ)り葉が一枚銀杏が桐にふんぞりかえる

Where is it this time?
Over our heads the light bulb
sways, lamplights flicker.

電球が頭上で揺れて灯光が揺らぐ今度はどこ？

A momentary
loss of balance, adjustment;
unmovingly moved.

バランスをふと失ってふと戻る動かずに動いて

Bare-branched sakura
along the Kanda River:
remembering spring.

裸ん坊の桜は春を覚えているよ神田川

My 5 year-old son,
a fever of 100,
midnight: such numbers.

五歳の息子七度八分深夜十二時の数字

That kitten's *nyyy-annn*:
from riverbank or river?
All I see is fish.

子猫鳴く岸かそれとも川？　見えるのは魚ばかり

And the numinous?
A stretch of flame-licked water
in autumn sunlight.

水面を舐めていく秋日の炎は恍惚と畏怖？

Whatever it is
the incinerator spews
reaches the river.

焼却炉の吐瀉物の正体は知らず川へ達する

The tree full of fruit:
there's a poem there somewhere,
by the oranges.

たわわに実る木のどこかに詩があって作者は蜜柑

A jigsaw puzzle,
figures upon the carpet:
half done; half undone.

ジグソーパズルはじゅうたんの柄半分完成半分は未完成

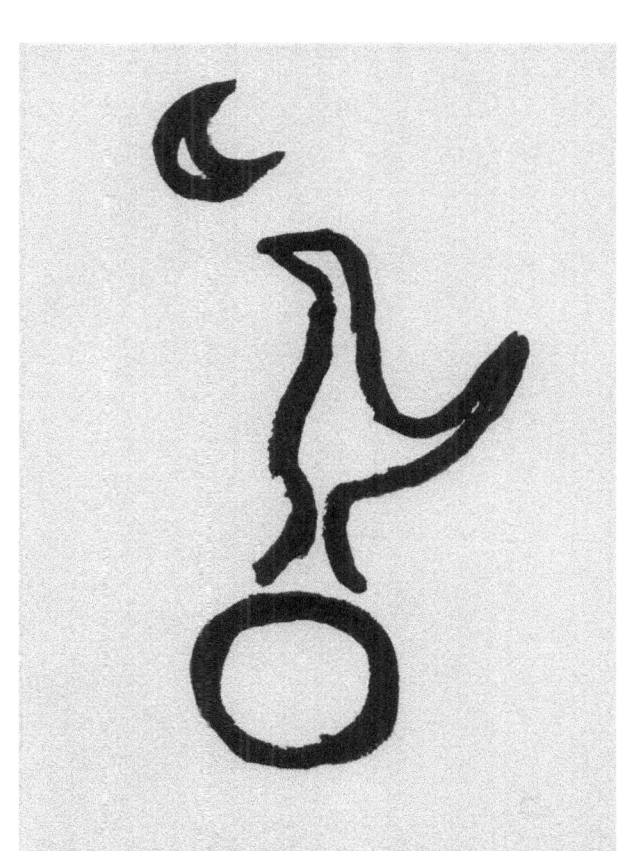

Afire on the head
that woman's hat, bright orange;
a fire in the head.

あの女人(ひと)の帽子橙(だいだい)頭にひとつ炎が灯る

In the school playground,
today's reading: .07
μSv/h

校庭に出て今日の読み取り

.07μSv/h

Combustible waste:
bonfires of the vanities.
Incombustible?

可燃性廃棄物は虚栄のかがり火もしかして不燃性?

GPS collars
on dosimetered monkeys;
petrified forests.

線量計測後猿どもにＧＰＳの首環あてがう森は石になった

Two helicopters;
a man hoovering up leaves;
Akatombo Park.

ヘリ二つ落ち葉吸い込む掃除機のひとがいて赤とんぼ公園

Inokashira:
by the river, under trees,
a young man shaving.

井の頭河畔の木陰で若い男が髭を剃っている

Those helicopters
approaching out of sunrise,
their thickening noise.

朝日を背にヘリコプターが向かってくる音轟音になる

The back of the house,
the still-in-leaf zelkova;
the lightening shade.

裏のケヤキはいまだ落葉せず蔭の色のみ薄らいできた

A lunar eclipse?
Strangers pour into the streets,
gaze as one, moonward.

月食の夜ふだん見かけない人々が通りに出て空を見上げている

The poisoned waters,
breast milk, baby formula;
the great star fallen.

汚染水母乳調合乳大きなお星様が落ちた

The princess tree's heart-
shaped leaves drawn by my daughter;
the Phoenix hidden.

娘が描く桐の葉のハートの形に鳳凰が潜む

Late afternoon light,
long shadows on yellowed grass
where the children play.

遅い午後の陽
黄色い草の長い影
子どもらが遊んでいる

In the bathwater
aromatic yuzu bob;
Toji: the solstice.

かぐわしい柚玉はしゃぐ冬至の湯船

Illuminations.
Mechanically produced:
on and off and on…

イルミネーションは機械仕掛けで点滅てんめつ……

Neon everywhere.
Light saturating the night.
Nowhere a shadow.

闇を浸すネオンの洪水夜はずぶ濡れて陰も無し

A sliver of moon;
how you smiled when the nurse asked
how you liked your tea.

看護士に茶の味を訊かれて微笑み返す糸の月

Celestial choirs
piped through the city's speakers;
our childhood's pattern.

天使の合唱がスピーカーから町へ―主は子どもたちのように

Telluric murmurs.
Ooze, seepage, liquefaction.
What was and will be.

地面がつぶやく染み出す液化するどうだったどうなるんだ

Three codgers and me,
watching the declining sun
define Mt Fuji.

三人のじいさんとわたし富士山を隈取る入り日を眺めつつ

Aboard a ghost train
through clockwork simulacra:
why are you crying?

幽霊列車から見えるのは時計仕掛けのニセモノなぜ泣くの？

Chance, circumstance, choice:
a butterfly-shaped brooch on
the floor of a train.

ふと見つけたがさてどうしよう電車の床に蝶のブローチ

Rain turning to snow
turning to rain via sleet;
the mulberry bush.

雨が雪へと変わりみぞれが雨となり桑の木に降る

'What Are Poets For?'...

Written in May 2011, in reply to a request from the Japan Mission Journal *for articles responding to the aftermath of the earthquake of 11 March 2011.*

Variations of Hölderlin's elegiac question, '*Wozu Dichter in dürftiger Zeit?* What are poets for in a time of need?' troubled the mind during the grim days that Japan recently traversed, and that continue in quiet mourning and worry. In the past, Japanese writers responded majestically to catastrophe, from 1212, when Kamo no Chōmei (鴨長明) penned his *Hōjōki* (The Ten Foot Square Hut), meditating on impermanence in a time of cataclysms, to 1965, when Ibuse Masuji (1898-1993) published *Kuroi Ame* (黒い雨, Black Rain), a dignified, probing response to the trauma of Hiroshima. Can poetry achieve a perspective on events that seem to destroy any meaningful perspective?

The Contemplation of Ruin

W. B. Yeats's play *The Resurrection* (1931) is dedicated to Junzo Sato, 'who gave me a sword,' the 'changeless' sword which in 'Meditations in Time of Civil War' helped Yeats 'moralise / [His] days out of their aimlessness'. Yeats's notes on the play, and the play itself, have begun to speak anew against the background of what we are learning to call the Great East Japan Earthquake, and its aftermath.

Yeats in the play casts his usual cold eye on the treadmill of historical change: 'Another Troy must rise and set, / Another lineage feed the crow'. But in the notes he recalls a wilder and more destructive attitude: 'When I was a boy everybody talked about progress, and rebellion against my elders took the form of aversion to that myth. I took satisfaction in certain public disasters, felt a sort of ecstasy at the contemplation of ruin'.

Yeats could be speaking of CNN, for whom, as recent weeks have taught us again, the worst news is the best news; or of the *schadenfreude* barely concealed in newspaper articles ostensibly concerned with the 'hubris' of building nuclear reactors in areas of potentially catastrophic seismic events.

Where there is hubris, nemesis cannot be far behind. Yeats continues, 'It seems to me of late that the sense of spiritual reality comes whether to the individual or to crowds from some violent shock, and that idea has the support of tradition'. To read such lines, and be pressed by circumstance to quote them, is to be struck once again by the indivisible combination of insight and absurdity in Yeats, to be caught up once again in the strange embrace of his acute observation and the uncanny sources of his speculative power.

Poets versus Theodicists

The Tokyo Governor, Shintaro Ishihara's March 14 comment that the earthquake was 'divine retribution' for the 'egotism' of modern Japan has support in the 'tradition' of grasping for a spiritual dimension to violent shock that Yeats evokes, the tradition of Sodom and Gomorrah, and the Flood, which Voltaire satirized in *Candide* and in his poem on the Lisbon earthquake of 1 November 1755. Was there really more vice and debauchery, Voltaire asked, among the people of Lisbon than in the great capitals of Europe, London and Paris? And as for the 'culpability' of Minamisanriku, Kamaishi, Kesennuma…?

That Nature has any interest at all in human affairs is an idea used for comic effect in Miroslav Holub's 'Man Cursing the Sea':

> Someone
> just climbed to the top of the cliff
> and started cursing the sea.

After suffering the man's mockery and abuse, the sea, abashed, licks the man's sandy footprints 'like a wounded dog':

And then he came down
and stroked
the small immense stormy mirror of the sea.

There you are, water, he said,
and went his way.

Though the luminous ironies of Holub's poem were darkened by renewed knowledge of the immensity of the sea's capacity for destruction, recollection of the poem's reversal of the power relations of the 'natural order' offered the solace of achieved perspective – so welcome, given the unrelievable, directionless despair induced by the images of devastation and the unrelenting battery of aftershocks which came in the hours and days following March 11. Perspective, as Joseph Brodsky once wrote, 'cuts emptiness deep and even.' But the task of achieving any kind of perspective at all amid the tumult of events took on the acuteness of dilemma as shocked relief at being spared gave way to the grim details emerging from Tohoku and as news from the nuclear reactors at Fukushima began to take on hallucinatory nightmarishness.

Distress and the Business of Living

Everything's a test. In the days following the earthquake, two poems of achieved and challenging perspective came to mind most often and most insistently: Czeslaw Milosz's 'Campo dei Fiori' and Yeats's 'Lapis Lazuli.' Fortifying words at a bewildering time, which themselves arose out of bewilderment and struggle amid historical calamity. Campo dei Fiori, the fruit market in Rome which was the site of the burning at the stake of Giordano Bruno in 1600, offers the speaker of Milosz's poem the solace of an historical focus for the pressing, unbearable awareness of the soul-fraying simultaneity of suffering and pleasure: at the same time and in the same locality one person suffers while others haggle, make love, go on with the business of living:

> In Rome on the Campo dei Fiori
> baskets of olives and lemons,
> cobbles spattered with wine
> and the wreckage of flowers.
> Vendors cover the trestles
> with rose-pink fish;
> armfuls of dark grapes
> heaped on peach-down.
>
> On this same square
> they burned Giordano Bruno.
> Henchmen kindled the pyre
> close-pressed by the mob.
> Before the flames had died
> the taverns were full again,
> baskets of olives and lemons
> again on the vendors' shoulders.

The poem was written at Easter, 1943, during the Warsaw Ghetto Uprising, an event that in its temporal and geographical co-incidence with the ordinary pleasures and continuing matter of everyday Warsaw life provokes and makes urgent the search for perspective:

> I thought of the Campo dei Fiori
> in Warsaw by the sky-carousel
> one clear spring evening
> to the strains of a carnival tune.
> The bright melody drowned
> the salvos from the ghetto wall,
> and couples were flying
> high in the cloudless sky.
>
> At times wind from the burning
> would drift dark kites along
> and riders on the carousel

> caught petals in midair.
> That same hot wind
> blew open the skirts of the girls
> and the crowds were laughing
> on that beautiful Warsaw Sunday.

In Tokyo, the same dilemma accompanied the daily chore of grocery shopping and insinuated itself into the debates over whether to proceed with pre-arranged events and everyday pleasures while people a short drive away struggled for life, and survivors made do in makeshift shelters without electricity and water, and without adequate food. The dark kites of the wind in the poem merged with that from the fires at the Cosmo petrochemical refinery in Ichihara, Chiba, and only too readily with the hot wind emerging out of Fukushima. But faced with the bleak, unsparing demand of such a question, what use was recalling a poem?

Yeats's Tragic Joy

Yeats's 'Lapis Lazuli' was written, like Milosz's poem, during a stricken historical moment – July 1936, amid upheaval in Spain and the fear of wider war in Europe – the intensities of the circumstances provoking a questioning of the efficacy of the 'superfluous' activity of art:

> I have heard that hysterical women say
> They are sick of the palette and fiddle-bow,
> Of poets that are always gay,
> For everybody knows or else should know
> That if nothing drastic is done
> Aeroplane and Zeppelin will come out,
> Pitch like King Billy bomb-balls in
> Until the town lie beaten flat.

Yeats's poem is the most strong-minded, invigorating response

I know to the debilitating suspicion of art's prerogatives and efficacy amid the onslaught of catastrophic event.

The poem came most forcefully and clarifyingly to mind on 20 March, when our university department went ahead with a reduced ceremony for the hundred or so of our students graduating this year. Trepidation at the emotional volatility of the occasion gave way to astonished admiration as these students, and colleagues, quietly acknowledged the shock and grief of events but offered each other, at least for that time spent together, a bright, sustaining companionship. In 'Lapis Lazuli' the line 'Gaiety transfiguring all that dread' could have been written with these people in mind.

Indeed much in Japanese culture strikes me as Yeatsian, though, as his dedication of *The Resurrection* to Junzo Sato implies, Yeats owed much to the 'custom and ceremony' of Japan, not least of which is the idea of the regenerative power of tumult. If the truth uttered out of the devastation wrought by the 'Galilean turbulence' of *The Resurrection* is one consequence of the violence of historical change – 'Everything that man esteems / Endures but a moment or a day' – in 'Lapis Lazuli' Yeats adds this more compelling, more challenging counter-truth, evoking the bright energy required for the necessary task of renewal that follows the potentially sapping inevitability of destruction: 'All things fall and are built again, / And those that build them again are gay'.

Myself and three friends drove to Tohoku on the weekend of May 13, to do volunteer work. In Kesennuma we cleared debris from a house that had been inundated. The house was big, 60 *tsubo* [200m^2], and had at one time roomed sailors working on the tuna fleet whose ships had been carried deep into the town by the tidal wave. The house had withstood the force of the water, but the flooding had destroyed everything inside. The owner, Goto-san, wanted all the heavy things he couldn't carry alone removed and placed on a slope behind the house, which was also part of his land. The four of us and Toriyama-san, our group leader, got down to work, and managed to get most of the job done by the time set for all volunteer work to finish, 3 PM. As we waited for the Volunteer Centre transport to arrive a young woman approached us. Like so many of the people we met that weekend, she thanked us for coming to help, and offered us water and snacks. Her name was Hiroko Sato, and she told us how, from the top floor of her workplace, she had watched her own house being carried away. She was staying in a house near Goto-san's now. She had lost everything; the clothes she was wearing given to her by friends. As she told us all of this, her voice was clear and strong, and the smile never left her face.

び築く者たちは陽気だ」。

私は三人の友人とボランティア活動をするために、五月一三日に車で東北に向かった。気仙沼で、私たちは一軒の浸水家屋から瓦礫を運び出す作業をした。それは六〇坪（二〇〇平米）もの大きな家で、以前はマグロ漁船団に乗り組む漁師たちの宿でもあったが、彼らの船は津波によって街の奥深くまで運ばれてしまっていた。家屋自体は水の力に耐え持ちこたえたものの、洪水は内部を全て破壊し尽くしていた。一人では到底運び出せない重い家具などを持ち出して、敷地の一部である裏の傾斜地に置いてくれるようにと家の持ち主である後藤さんが言った。私たち四人と、グループ・リーダーである鳥山さんとで、早速仕事に取りかかった。そして、ボランティア・センターからの迎えが到着するのを待つ間に、なんとかほとんどの仕事を終えることができた。あの週末出会った多くの人々がそうであったように、彼女は、手伝いにきてくれてありがとう、と礼を述べ、私たちに水とスナックをふるまってくれた。

彼女の名は佐藤寛子、あの日、職場の最上階から自分の家が津波にさらわれていくのを見ていた時のことを語ってくれた。今は、後藤さんの家の近くの家にお世話になっていますが、全てを無くしました。今着ているのも友達のくれた服なんです。こう話しながらも、彼女の声は明瞭で、力強く、その顔から微笑みが絶えることはなかった。

（翻訳：大野 光子）

飛行機やツェッペリンが現れて、ビリー王みたいに炸裂弾を投げつけて、町を叩きつぶしてしまうのは誰もが知っているし、知っていなけりゃならないこと。

イェイツの詩は、大惨事に遇っている最中の芸術の特権や有効性についての萎えそうな疑念に対し、私の知る限り、最も断固たる、かつ元気付ける応答である。この詩は三月二〇日に、実に力強く、明快な形で心に浮かんだのだが、それは勤務する大学の学科が、一〇〇人余りの卒業生たちのために簡略な式を挙行した日のことであった。卒業式という感傷的不安定さを抱えた場で抱いた心の動揺は、やがて驚きを含んだ賞讃に変わった。というのも、学生たちや同僚たちは静かに一連の出来事の衝撃や悲しみを語ったのだが、少なくとも一緒にいる間は、互いに明るく支え合う交流をしていたからだ。「ラピス・ラズリ」には、「陽気さが恐怖をそっくり変えてしまうのだ」という一行があるが、このような人々を念頭に置いて、これは書かれたのではなかったか。

確かに、日本文化の中にはイェイツ的だと感じさせるものがあるとしばしば気付かされる。『復活』が佐藤淳造に捧げられていること自体が示唆するように、イェイツは日本の「慣習と典礼」に多くを負っているが、中でも特に、大惨事のもつ再生力、という考え方がそうだ。もし、『復活』の「ガリラヤの騒乱」によって引き起こされた荒廃に発する真理が、歴史的変換——「人間が尊ぶすべてのものは／一瞬あるいは一日の命しかない」——の凶暴性がもたらす結果のひとつであるとするなら、「ラピス・ラズリ」で再生の役割を果たすに必須の明るさに満ちたエネルギーを書き加えている。力を弱めかねない必然的な破壊に続いて、「すべての事物は崩壊し、また構築される／そうして、ふたたびそれを示しているのだ。「すべての事物は崩壊し、また構築される／そうして、ふたたび呼び起こすことによって、

あの　美しいワルシャワの日曜日

東京では、同様のジレンマが毎日の食料品の買い出しにも付きまとっていた。ほんの少し車を走らせるだけで行ける距離に、苦労して生き延びようとしている人々がおり、被災者たちがなんとか間に合わせの避難所で、電気も水道もなく、充分な食料も確保できずやり繰りしている一方で、既に決まっていた事柄や日常の娯楽は進めていこうではないかという議論の中にも、このジレンマはいつのまにか入り込んだ。さらに福島から吹き出す熱い風とも難なく重ねて考えることができた。しかし、このような疑念を冷酷無慈悲にも突きつけられた状況において、詩を思い出すことは何の役に立ったというのか？

イェイツの悲劇的歓喜

イェイツの「ラピス・ラズリ」は、ミウォシュの詩と同様、一九三六年七月、スペイン内乱とヨーロッパ内の広域戦争の不安の中でのことだった。状況の切迫が、「無用な」芸術活動の有効性を問う態度を引き起こしていたのだ。

ヒステリックな女たちがこう言うのを聞いた。パレットも、ヴァイオリンの弓も、いつも陽気な詩人たちも、もうたくさん。思い切った手を打たないと、

やワルシャワの日常の中で続く事柄と時間的かつ地理的に重ねられていること自体、何がしかの展望を得たいという切迫した思いに駆り立てられていたことを想起させる。

カンポ・デ・フィオーリ広場のことを
ワルシャワの空中回転木馬の脇で
カーニバル調の曲につられて考えたのは
ある晴れた春の夕べ
ゲットーの壁から聞こえる一斉射撃の音を
明るいメロディーが遮り
連れ立った男女が　高く
舞い上がっていた　雲ひとつない空

時には　炎の巻き起こす風が
暗色の凧を　近くまで漂わせ
回転木馬の乗り手たちは
上空で　花びらを拾った
まさに　その熱い風が
少女たちのスカートを膨らませ
群衆は　笑いさざめいていた

ローマのカンポ・デ・フィオーリ広場
オリーブやレモンの篭
ワインの飛び散った石畳
花々の残骸
商い人たちは架台の上
一面に　ローズピンクの魚を並べ
幾抱えもの濃い色の葡萄が
桃の綿毛の上に積み上がる

まさにこの広場で
ジョルダーノ・ブルーノが火炙りに
取り巻きたちが　群衆に押され
火刑柱に火を放った
焔が燃え尽きる前に
居酒屋はふたたび一杯
オリーブとレモンの篭も
商い人たちの肩の上

この詩は、一九四三年の復活祭、ワルシャワのゲットー蜂起時に書かれたもので、この出来事が、ありふれた喜び

ホルブの詩の明るいアイロニーは、今回改めて思い知らされた海の破壊力の彫大さによって暗く変わってしまったにせよ、この詩が「自然界の秩序」に添った力関係を逆転させたことを思い出して、私には何とか到達できた展望という意味での慰藉が得られた。数々の荒廃のイメージや、三月一一日以後何時間も何日も続いた容赦ない余震の連続によって引き起こされた、癒すこともを向かうべき方向も見えない絶望の中で、それはひどくありがたい慰藉だった。かつてヨシフ・ブロツキーが書いたように、展望は「空虚さを深く均一に切断する」。だが、次々と起る異常な事態の中にあって、どのような種類のであれ何らかの展望に到達することは、激しいジレンマを感じさせることもあった。被害に遭わずに済んだという衝動的な安堵感は、やがて東北から伝えられる詳細な報告によって暗澹たる気持ちへと転じ、福島原発からのニュースが、幻覚を生み出しかねない悪夢のような恐怖を帯び始めたからである。

悲嘆、そして生きていくこと

何事も試練である。大震災後の日々、達戒されたとはいえ困難な展望を提示する二つの詩が、他の何にも増して頻繁に、私の頭に浮かんできた。チェスワフ・ミウォシュの「カンポ・デ・フィオーリ」とイェイツの「ラピス・ラズリ」である。それらの詩自体が歴史的な危機の最中に困惑と苦闘の中から生まれたがゆえに、困惑する時期の私の精神に活力を与えてくれる詩の言葉だった。「カンポ・デ・フィオーリ」はローマの集物市場で、一六〇〇年にジョルダーノ・ブルーノが火刑に処された場所だが、歴史に焦点を当てることによって、差し迫る、堪え難い、魂をすり減らすような苦痛と悦楽を同時に感受しつつ、ミウォシュの詩の語り手は慰藉を得る。同じ時に、しかも同じ場所で、一人は苦しみに遇う一方、他の人々は値切りあったり、愛しあったりして、生き続けているのだから。

見いだすことができる。それは、ソドムとゴモラや、大洪水の伝承のことであり、ヴォルテールが『カンディド』や一七五五年一一月一日のリスボン地震について書いた詩の中で諷刺している伝承のことである。リスボンの人々の間には、本当にヨーロッパの大都市、ロンドンやパリに勝るほどの悪徳や堕落が蔓延していたのだろうか、とヴォルテールは問う。さらに言うなら、南三陸や釜石や気仙沼が犯した「過失」とは・・・？人間界の出来事に、自然はいかほどでも関心があるのかという疑問は、ミロスラフ・ホルブの詩「海を呪う男」の中で、コミカルに表現されている。

誰かが

断崖を登り、てっぺんに辿り着いて

海を呪う言葉を叫び始める

男の嘲笑や罵りに耐えた後、海は当惑し、「傷ついた犬のように」、砂に刻まれた男の足跡を舐めるのだ。

そして それから 彼は降りて来て

ちっぽけで広大な 嵐を含んだ鏡のような海を

撫でた

よしよし 海よ と言って

もと来た道を 戻っていった

劇中で、イェイツは歴史の転換期の足踏みに、いつも通りの冷たい視線を投げかける。「再びトロイの城が興って滅びねばならぬ／再び王の家系が鴉の餌にならねばならぬ」。しかし、注の中では、彼はもっと荒々しく破壊的な態度も想起している。「私の少年時代には、誰もが進歩について語っていた。年長者に対する私の反抗は、その進歩神話を毛嫌いする形をとったのだが、それは、人々に降り掛かった災難を満足に感じたり、廃墟を凝視することにより、ある種の恍惚感を得るといったものだった」。イェイツのこの発言は、あたかもCNNについて述べているかのようだ。というのも、最近の数週間が改めて思い知らせてくれたように、メディアにとって、ニュースというのは事態が酷ければ酷いほど価値があるからだ。あるいは、大惨事を引き起こす可能性のある連続的地震発生地域に原子力発電所を建造しようとする「傲慢不遜な態度」を懸念するかのような新聞記事の下に、隠そうとしても現れる「他人の不幸を喜ぶ気持ち」についても、彼は述べているかのようである。

傲慢さのあるところには、遠からず天罰が訪れる。イェイツは、続いて、こう述べている。「最近思うのだが、精神的な現実感というのは、個人であれ集団に対してであれ、何らかの強烈な衝撃によってもたらされるものである。そしてこの考えは、伝承の中に裏付けを見いだすことができる」。このような文章を読み、そして状況の要請により、さらにこれを引用せざるを得なくなってみると、イェイツの中に分ち難く渾在する見識と不合理に改めて驚かされる。つまり、鋭敏な洞察の力と、推論的な力の神秘的とも思える源泉が、イェイツの中で不可思議なまでに渾然一体こなっていることに今更ながら気付かされるのである。

詩人対神義論者

　石原慎太郎東京都知事が、大震災は現代日本の「我欲」に対する「天罰」であるとした三月一四日の発言は、確かに、イェイツの言うところの強烈な衝撃の中で精神的な拠り所を求めようとする古来の「伝承」の中に、根拠を

75

「詩人は何のために？」…

この一文は、二〇一一年三月一一日に発生した大震災への反応について書くようにとの『ジャパン・ミッション・ジャーナル』の依頼に応えて、二〇一一年五月に書いたものである。

最近日本が遭遇した暗澹たる日々、そして今も続く静かな哀悼の思いと不安の中で、ヘルダーリンの嘆きの問い「乏しい時代に詩人は何のためにあるか？」が、私の心を悩ませていた。日本の文筆家たちは、過去において、鴨長明が『方丈記』で地殻変動の最中に無常について思いを巡らせた一二一二年から、井伏鱒二（一八九八―一九九三）が広島のトラウマへの堂々かつ徹底的な応答として『黒い雨』を刊行した一九六五年にいたるまで、大災害に際し威厳ある対応をしてきた。果たして詩は、意義ある展望のすべてを破壊し去ったかに見える今回の連続的惨事に対峙して、何ほどかの展望に到達することができるのだろうか？

廃墟についての思索

W・B・イェイツの戯曲『復活』（一九三一）は、「一振りの日本刀を贈ってくれた」佐藤淳造氏に捧げられており、「内戦時代の省察」という詩の中で書かれているように、その「不滅の」刀は「日々が漫然と過ぎてゆくのを正し／訓戒を与え」てくれたとイェイツは言う。イェイツ自身による戯曲の注、そして戯曲自体は、私たちが東日本大震災と呼ぶことに慣れつつある今回の大災害とその余波を背景に置いて見るとき、新たなメッセージを語り始めたようだ。

www.ingramcontent.com/pod-product-compliance
Lightning Source LLC
Chambersburg PA
CBHW031212090426
42736CB00009B/878